Parabéns!
Agora você faz parte do **Plurall**, a plataforma digital do seu livro didático! Acesse e conheça todos os recursos e funcionalidades disponíveis para as suas aulas digitais.

Baixe o aplicativo do **Plurall** para Android e IOS ou acesse www.plurall.net e cadastre-se utilizando o seu código de acesso exclusivo:

CB027772

AAAA32ZA4

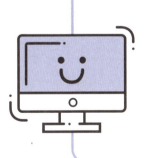

Este é o seu código de acesso Plurall. Cadastre-se e ative-o para ter acesso aos conteúdos relacionados a esta obra.

 @plurallnet

 @plurallnetoficial

COLE OS ADESIVOS NA CAPA DO LIVRO.

ENSINO FUNDAMENTAL • ANOS INICIAIS

Eliete Canesi Morino

Graduada em Língua e Literatura Inglesa e Tradução e Interpretação pela Pontifícia Universidade Católica de São Paulo (PUC-SP).

Especialização em Língua Inglesa pela International Bell School of London.

Pós-graduada em Metodologia da Língua Inglesa pela Faculdade de Tecnologia e Ciência (FTC-SP).

Atuou como professora da rede particular de ensino e em projetos comunitários.

Rita Brugin de Faria

Graduada pela Faculdade de Arte Santa Marcelina e pela Faculdade Paulista de Arte, ambas em São Paulo (SP).

Especialização em Língua Inglesa pela International Bell School of London.

Pós-graduada em Metodologia da Língua Inglesa pela Faculdade de Tecnologia e Ciência (FTC-SP).

Especialista em alfabetização, atuou como professora e coordenadora pedagógica das redes pública e particular de ensino.

Áudios

Escaneie o *QR Code* para ter acesso aos áudios deste volume e do *reader* que o acompanha.

Presidência: Mario Ghio Júnior
Vice-presidência de educação digital: Camila Montero Vaz Cardoso
Direção editorial: Lidiane Vivaldini Olo
Gerência editorial: Julio Cesar Augustus de Paula Santos
Coordenação editorial: Luciana Nicoleti
Edição: Ana Lucia Militello
Aprendizagem digital: Renata Galdino (ger.), Beatriz de Almeida Pinto Rodrigues da Costa (coord. de Experiência de aprendizagem), Carla Isabel Ferreira Reis (coord. de Produção multimídia), Daniela dos Santos Di Nubila (coord. de Produção digital), Rogerio Fabio Alves (coord. de Publicação), Vanessa Tavares Menezes de Souza (coord. de Design digital)
Planejamento e controle de produção: Flávio Matuguma (ger.), Juliana Batista (coord.) e Jayne Ruas (analista)
Revisão: Letícia Pieroni (coord.), Aline Cristina Vieira, Anna Clara Razvickas, Carla Bertinato, Daniela Lima, Danielle Modesto, Diego Carbone, Elane Vicente, Kátia S. Lopes Godoi, Lilian M. Kumai, Malvina Tomáz, Marília H. Lima, Patricia Rocco S. Renda, Paula Freire, Paula Rubia Baltazar, Paula Teixeira, Raquel A. Taveira, Ricardo Miyake, Shirley Figueiredo Ayres, Tayra Alfonso e Thaise Rodrigues
Arte: Fernanda Costa e Silva (ger.), Catherine Saori Ishihara (coord.) e Karina Vizeu Winkaler (edição de arte)
Diagramação: Ilê Comunicação Eireli
Iconografia e tratamento de imagem: Roberta Bento (ger.), Claudia Bertolazzi (coord.), Roberta Freire Lacerda dos Santos (pesquisa iconográfica), Iron Mantovanello Oliveira e Fernanda Crevin (tratamento de imagens)
Licenciamento de conteúdo de terceiros: Roberta Bento (ger.), Jenis Oh (coord.) e Liliane Rodrigues (analista de licenciamento)
Ilustrações: Clau Souza, Estudio Ornitorrinco, Ilustra Cartoon, Marcos Mello, Sirayama e Superludico
Cartografia: Eric Fuzii (coord.) e Robson da Rocha (edição de arte)
Design: Erik Taketa (coord.) e Talita Guedes da Silva (capa e proj. gráfico)
Ilustração da capa e logotipo: Superludico

Todos os direitos reservados por Somos Sistemas de Ensino S.A.
Avenida Paulista, 901, 6º andar – Bela Vista
São Paulo – SP – CEP 01310-200
http://www.somoseducacao.com.br

Dados Internacionais de Catalogação na Publicação (CIP)

```
Faria, Rita Brugin de
   Hello! Kids 1º ano / Rita Brugin de Faria, Eliete Canesi
Morino. -- 6. ed. -- São Paulo : Ática, 2023.

Suplementado pelo manual do professor.
Bibliografia
ISBN 978-85-0819-859-7 (aluno)
ISBN 978-85-0819-853-5 (professor)

1. Língua inglesa (Ensino fundamental) I. Morino, Eliete
Canesi II. Título

22-0173                                         CDD 372.652
```

Angélica Ilacqua – Bibliotecária – CRB-8/7057

2023
6ª edição
3ª impressão
De acordo com a BNCC.

Impressão e acabamento: EGB Editora Gráfica Bernardi Ltda.

Uma publicação

Dados Internacionais de Catalogação na Publicação (CIP)

```
Faria, Rita Brugin de
   Hello! Kids 1º ano [livro eletrônico] / Rita Brugin de
Faria, Eliete Canesi Morino. - 1. ed. -- São Paulo : Ática,
2023.
   PDF

Suplementado pelo manual do professor.
Bibliografia
ISBN 978-85-0819-849-8 (e-book) (aluno)
ISBN 978-85-0819-844-3 (e-book) (professor)

1. Língua inglesa (Ensino fundamental) I. Morino, Eliete
Canesi II. Título

22-0178                                         CDD 372.652
```

Angélica Ilacqua – Bibliotecária – CRB-8/7057

2022

WELCOME, STUDENTS!

LET'S LEARN ENGLISH WITH HELLO! KIDS 1

CONTENTS

	CONTEMPORARY THEMES (CT) AND ENGLISH LANGUAGE COMPETENCES (ELC)	CONTENTS	VALUES	TIME TO LEARN ABOUT (CLIL)
WELCOME! (MEET THE CHARACTERS!) P. 6	VIDA FAMILIAR E SOCIAL	• HI! HELLO! • I'M… • WHO IS THIS? • THIS IS… • WELCOME, MEET THE CHARACTERS!	FAMILY TIES AND FRIENDSHIP	—
UNIT 1 MY FAMILY (BROWN FAMILY MEMBERS) P. 8	VIDA FAMILIAR E SOCIAL. RESPEITO E VALORIZAÇÃO DO IDOSO ELC: GENERAL: 2 / SPECIFIC: 3 / ENGLISH LANGUAGE: 2	• BABY BROTHER, BROTHER, DAD, DOG (FIDO), FAMILY, GRANDMA, GRANDPA, MOM, SISTER, ROBOT (KIDDIE5). • HELLO! • THIS IS (MY FAMILY). • IS THIS (LEO)? YES. / NO. • I LOVE MY FAMILY.	RESPECT	FAMILIES (SOCIAL STUDIES/ MATH/ART)
UNIT 2 WELCOME, TEACHER! (SCHOOL OBJECTS, GREETING THE TEACHER AND STUDENTS) P. 16	VIDA FAMILIAR E SOCIAL ELC: GENERAL: 2 / SPECIFIC: 3 / ENGLISH LANGUAGE: 1	• BOOK, CRAYON, ERASER, PENCIL, SCHOOLBAG, STUDENT, TEACHER. • GREETINGS: GOOD MORNING, GOOD AFTERNOON. • WELCOME, TEACHER! • I'M (A STUDENT). • YOU'RE (A TEACHER). • THIS IS (A PENCIL). • IS IT (A CRAYON)? YES. / NO.	COOPERATE	—

REVIEW FROM UNITS 1 AND 2   P. 24

UNIT 3 ART CLASS (COLORS) P. 26	VIDA FAMILIAR E SOCIAL ELC: GENERAL: 2 / ENGLISH LANGUAGE: 1	• ART, BLUE, BROWN, GREEN, ORANGE, PINK, RED, YELLOW. • WHAT COLOR IS THIS?/IT'S (GREEN). • I LOVE (YELLOW)!	DO YOUR BEST!	COLORS (SCIENCE/ART)
UNIT 4 LET'S PLAY HOPSCOTCH! (NUMBERS 1 TO 10 AND PLAYGROUND TOYS) P. 34	VIDA FAMILIAR E SOCIAL	• ONE, TWO, THREE, FOUR, FIVE, SIX, SEVEN, EIGHT, NINE, TEN; SEESAW, SLIDE, SWING. • BREAK TIME. • IT'S MY TURN! • LET'S PLAY! • LET'S COUNT!	KEEP CALM!	—

REVIEW FROM UNITS 3 AND 4   P. 42

UNIT 5 SHOW ME YOUR ARMS (BODY PARTS) P. 44	SAÚDE ELC: GENERAL: 2 / SPECIFIC: 3 / ENGLISH LANGUAGE: 2	• ARM, FOOT, HAND, HEAD, LEG, SCIENCE TEACHER. • SHOW ME… • TOUCH YOUR…	NO PREJUDICE	MY BODY (SCIENCE/P.E., PHYSICAL EDUCATION)

4 FOUR

UNIT	CONTEMPORARY THEMES (CT) AND ENGLISH LANGUAGE COMPETENCES (ELC)	CONTENTS	VALUES	TIME TO LEARN ABOUT (CLIL)
UNIT 6 **AT THE PARK** (NATURE) P. 52	EDUCAÇÃO AMBIENTAL E SAÚDE	• BIRD, BUTTERFLY, CAT, DOG, FLOWER, ICE CREAM, KITE, PARK, TREE. • THIS ICE CREAM IS DELICIOUS! • WHAT IS THIS? IT'S A/AN… • WHAT COLOR…? IT'S…	RESPECT NATURE	—

REVIEW FROM UNITS 5 AND 6   P. 60

UNIT	CONTEMPORARY THEMES (CT) AND ENGLISH LANGUAGE COMPETENCES (ELC)	CONTENTS	VALUES	TIME TO LEARN ABOUT (CLIL)
UNIT 7 **THE GREEN CAP** (CLOTHES AND SHOES) P. 62	EDUCAÇÃO PARA O CONSUMO. EDUCAÇÃO EM DIREITOS HUMANOS ELC: GENERAL: 2 / SPECIFIC: 3 AND 4 / ENGLISH LANGUAGE: 3	• CAP, DRESS, MALL, PANTS, SNEAKERS, SOCKS, T-SHIRT. • WHAT IS THIS? IT'S A/AN… • WHAT COLOR IS IT? IT'S…	SOLIDARITY	CLOTHES (SOCIAL STUDIES/SCIENCE)
UNIT 8 **I LIKE COOKIES!** (FOOD AND DRINKS) P. 70	EDUCAÇÃO PARA O CONSUMO. EDUCAÇÃO AMBIENTAL. EDUCAÇÃO ALIMENTAR E NUTRICIONAL	• APPLE, BANANA, CHOCOLATE, COOKIES, EGGS, JUICE, MILK, SUPERMARKET. • DO YOU LIKE…? • I LIKE… • I DON'T LIKE…	NO FOOD WASTE!	—

REVIEW FROM UNITS 7 AND 8   P. 78

UNIT	CONTEMPORARY THEMES (CT) AND ENGLISH LANGUAGE COMPETENCES (ELC)	CONTENTS	VALUES	TIME TO LEARN ABOUT (CLIL)
UNIT 9 **AT THE BEACH** (BEACH ELEMENTS) P. 80	EDUCAÇÃO AMBIENTAL ELC: GENERAL: 7 / SPECIFIC: 3 AND 4 / ENGLISH LANGUAGE: 2	• BEACH, BOAT, BUCKET, FISH, SAND, SEA, SEASHELL, SHOVEL, SKY, STARFISH, SUN. • IT'S SUMMER! • IT'S A BEAUTIFUL DAY! • WHERE IS…? / IT'S HERE.	PROTECT THE OCEAN	OCEANS (SCIENCE/ART)
UNIT 10 **ON THE FARM** (FARM ANIMALS) P. 88	EDUCAÇÃO AMBIENTAL	• CHICKS, COW, DUCK, FARM, HEN, HORSE, PIG. • WHERE IS THE…? • IT'S HERE / IT'S OVER THERE.	PROTECT THE ANIMALS	—

REVIEW FROM UNITS 9 AND 10   P. 96

- PROJECTS P. 98
- PICTURE DICTIONARY P. 102
- WORKBOOK P. 107
- CELEBRATION SONGS P. 127
- CELEBRATION CRAFTS P. 129
  - HAPPY EASTER! P. 129
  - MOTHER'S DAY P. 131
  - FATHER'S DAY P. 133
- FRIENDSHIP DAY P. 133
- THANKSGIVING DAY P. 135
- CHRISTMAS P. 137
- GAMES P. 139
  - MEMORY GAME P. 139
  - MINI CARDS P. 141
- STICKERS P. 149

ICONS

 ACT OUT
 CHECK
 CIRCLE
 COLOR
 COUNT
 CUT
 DRAW
 GLUE
 LET'S TALK
 LISTEN
 MAKE AN X
 MATCH
 NUMBER
 POINT
 READ
 SAY
 SING
 STICK
 WORKBOOK
 WRITE

WELCOME! MEET THE CHARACTERS!

1. LISTEN, POINT AND SAY.

2. LISTEN, STICK AND SAY!

BABY BROTHER   MOM   SISTER

DAD   DOG (FIDO)   BROTHER

GRANDPA   GRANDMA

3. LISTEN AND MAKE AN X.

A)

B)

C)

TO LEARN MORE

GRANDMA = GRANDMOTHER
GRANDPA = GRANDFATHER

LET'S SING!

I LOVE MY FAMILY!

FAMILY IS EVERYTHING,
MAYBE BIG,
MAYBE SMALL.
FAMILY IS LOVE,
AND LOVE IS EVERYTHING!

4. MAKE AN **X** IN THE BIG FAMILY.

Say with Me!
I'M GRATEFUL TO MY GRANDMA AND MY GRANDPA. MY BIG FAMILY.

GROWING UP

RESPECT

5. LOOK AT THE PICTURE AND TALK TO YOUR CLASSMATES.

6. DRAW YOUR FAMILY AND GIVE IT TO YOUR GRANDMA AND GRANDPA.

CHECK YOUR PROGRESS

TIME TO LEARN ABOUT FAMILIES

IS YOUR FAMILY BIG OR SMALL?

1. LOOK AT THE PICTURES. THEN DRAW YOUR FAMILY.

A)

B)

C)

D)

NOW, MY FAMILY AND ME!

2. LOOK AT THIS TIMELINE. THEN DRAW YOUR OWN.

UNIT 2

WELCOME, TEACHER!

1. LISTEN, POINT AND SAY.

2. LISTEN, STICK AND SAY!

18 EIGHTEEN

3. LISTEN AND DRAW.

4. LOOK, CIRCLE AND SAY.

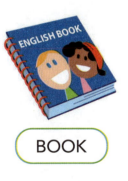
BOOK

PENCIL

SCHOOLBAG

ERASER

CRAYON

5. LET'S ACT OUT!

A) COME TO THE BOARD.

B) PLEASE, OPEN YOUR BOOKS.

C) EXCUSE ME!

D) SAY "WELCOME, TEACHER!".

LET'S SING!

I'M SO VERY HAPPY!

GOOD MORNING, DEAR FRIEND!
GOOD MORNING, HOW ARE YOU?
I'M SO VERY HAPPY,
TO SAY HELLO TO YOU!
GOOD AFTERNOON, DEAR FRIEND!
GOOD AFTERNOON, HOW ARE YOU?
I'M SO VERY HAPPY,
TO SAY HELLO TO YOU!

6. NUMBER THE SEQUENCE.

Say with Me!

THAT'S A TALL, TALL TEACHER!

GROWING UP

COOPERATE

7. LOOK AT THE PICTURE AND TALK TO YOUR CLASSMATES.

8. THINK OF COOPERATION ATTITUDES. DRAW ONE AND ACT IT OUT.

CHECK YOUR PROGRESS

AWESOME!   GOOD JOB!   I CAN DO BETTER.

REVIEW

1. LOOK AT THE MAZE. LET'S HELP LEO FIND HIS FAMILY.

2. CHECK THE SCHOOL OBJECTS.

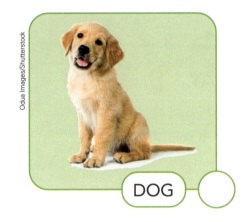
DOG

SCHOOLBAG

ERASER

PENCIL

CRAYONS

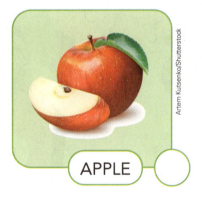
APPLE

MILK

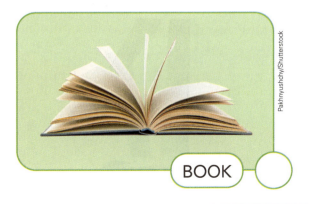
BOOK

TWENTY-FIVE 25

UNIT

3 ART CLASS

1. LISTEN, POINT AND SAY.

2. LISTEN, STICK AND SAY!

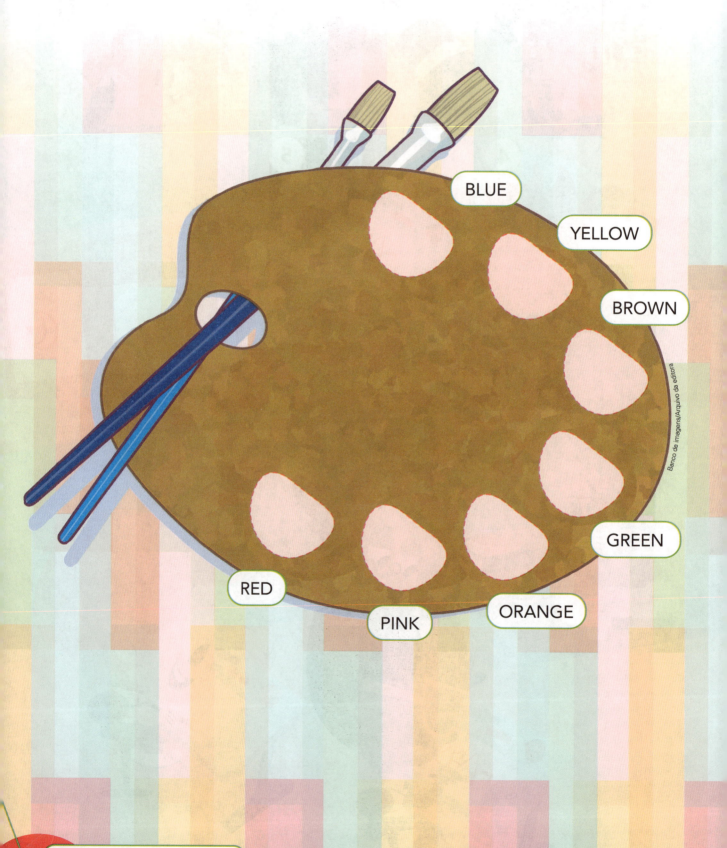

28 TWENTY-EIGHT

3. LISTEN AND MAKE AN **X**.

A)

B)

C)

LET'S SING!

RAP OF THE COLORS

RED, PINK AND BLUE,
RED, PINK AND BLUE.
WHAT COLOR IS THE SKY?
IT'S BLUE! IT'S BLUE!
GREEN, YELLOW, RED,
GREEN, YELLOW, RED.
WHAT COLOR IS THE APPLE?
IT'S RED, IT'S RED.

4. SING AND COLOR.

Say with Me!
ONE SQUARE, TWO CIRCLES, TWO CIRCLES AND THREE TRIANGLES.

GROWING UP

DO YOUR BEST!

5. LOOK AT THE PICTURE AND TALK TO YOUR CLASSMATES.

6. DRAW TWO FACES IN THE PAPER: A SMILING AND A SAD FACE.

CHECK YOUR PROGRESS

AWESOME!

GOOD JOB!

I CAN DO BETTER.

THIRTY-ONE 31

TIME TO LEARN ABOUT

COLORS

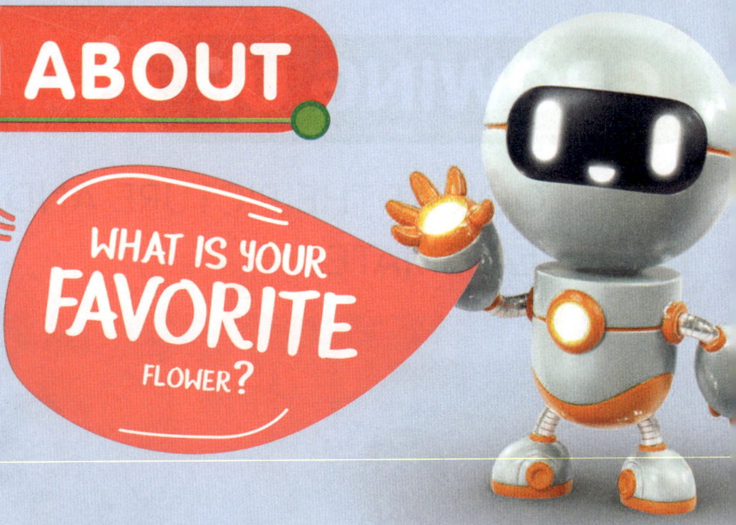

WHAT IS YOUR
FAVORITE
FLOWER?

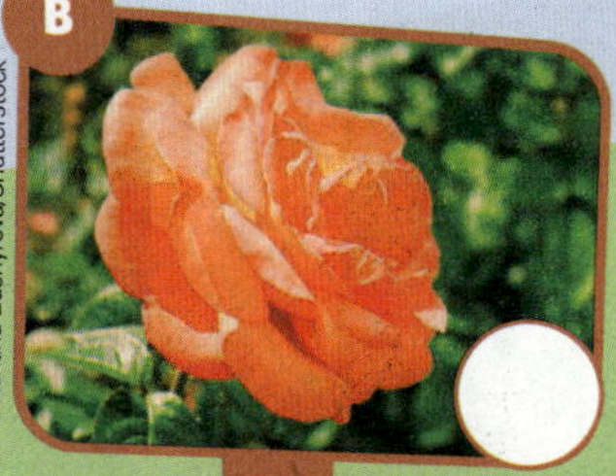

1. LOOK AT THE FLOWERS AND MAKE AN **X**.

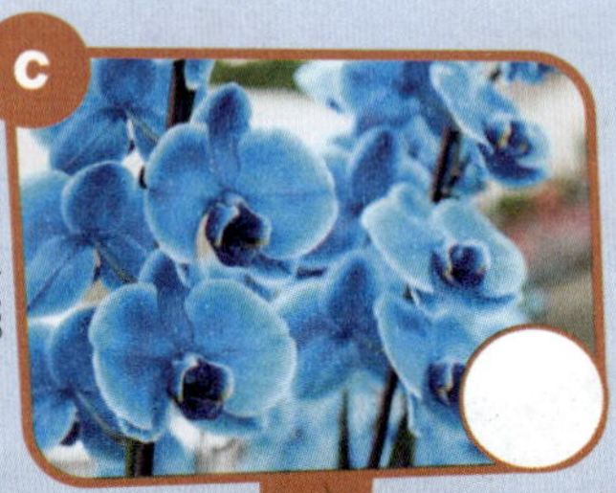

A

Serhii Brovko/Shutterstock

B

Roxana Bashyrova/Shutterstock

C

CoolR/Shutterstock

D

Eva Kristin Almqvist/Shutterstock

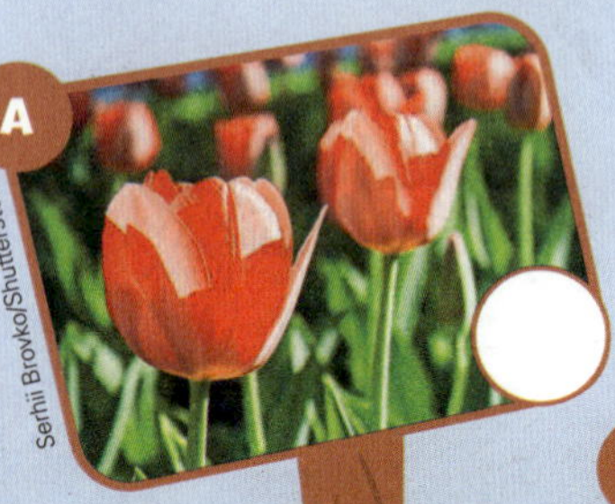

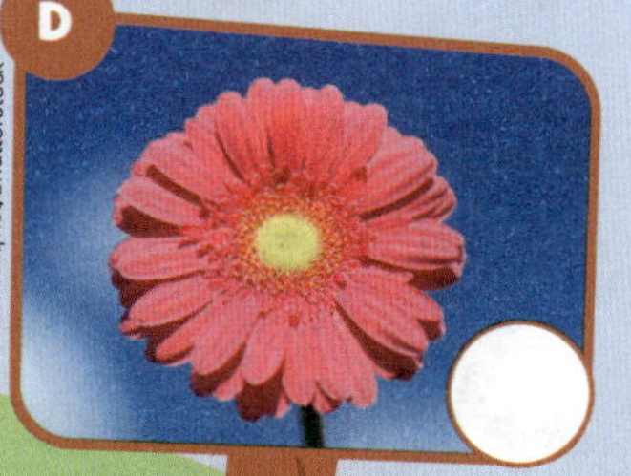

2. LOOK AND MATCH THE PARTS OF THE SUNFLOWER.

Ilustra Cartoon/Arquivo da editora

- LEAF
- PETALS
- ROOT
- STEM

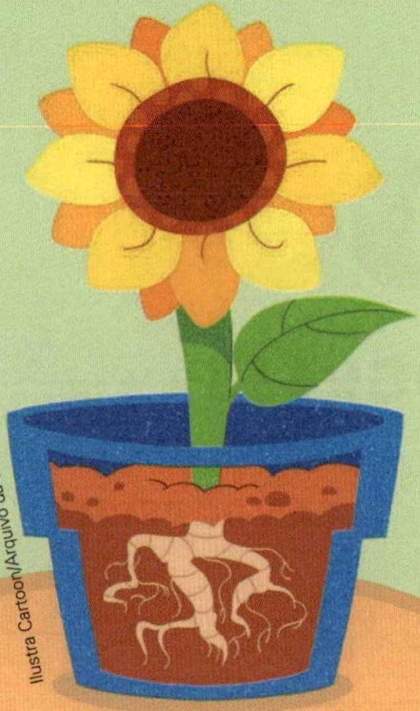

3. LOOK AND MATCH.

 1   2   3

THIS IS MY COLORFUL GARDEN!

4. LOOK AT THE GARDEN. DRAW AND COLOR YOUR FAVORITE FLOWERS.

2. LISTEN, STICK AND SAY!

Say with Me!
HOP, HOP, HOP! LET'S PLAY HOPSCOTCH. WATCH, WATCH!

3. LISTEN AND CIRCLE.

A)

B)

C)

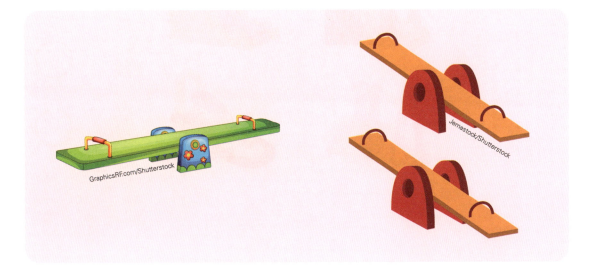

4. COUNT AND MAKE AN X.

A)

B)

C)

5. COUNT AND COLOR THE GRAPH.

	1	2	3	4	5	6
seesaw						
ball						
slide						
swing						

THIRTY-NINE 39

LET'S SING!

SAY IT AGAIN!

ONE, TWO, PUT ON YOUR SHOE.
THREE, FOUR, CLOSE THE DOOR.
FIVE, SIX, PICK UP STICKS.
SEVEN, EIGHT, EAT OFF A PLATE.
NINE, TEN, SAY IT AGAIN.

6. SING AND NUMBER.

GROWING UP

KEEP CALM!

7. LOOK AT THE PICTURE AND TALK TO YOUR CLASSMATES.

8. WHAT DO YOU DO TO KEEP YOURSELF CALM?

CHECK YOUR PROGRESS

AWESOME!   GOOD JOB!   I CAN DO BETTER.

REVIEW

1. COLOR BY NUMBER.

2. MATCH.

A)  — SIX

B)  — THREE

C)  — FOUR

D)  — EIGHT

E)  — SEVEN

UNIT 5
SHOW ME YOUR ARMS

1. LISTEN, POINT AND SAY.

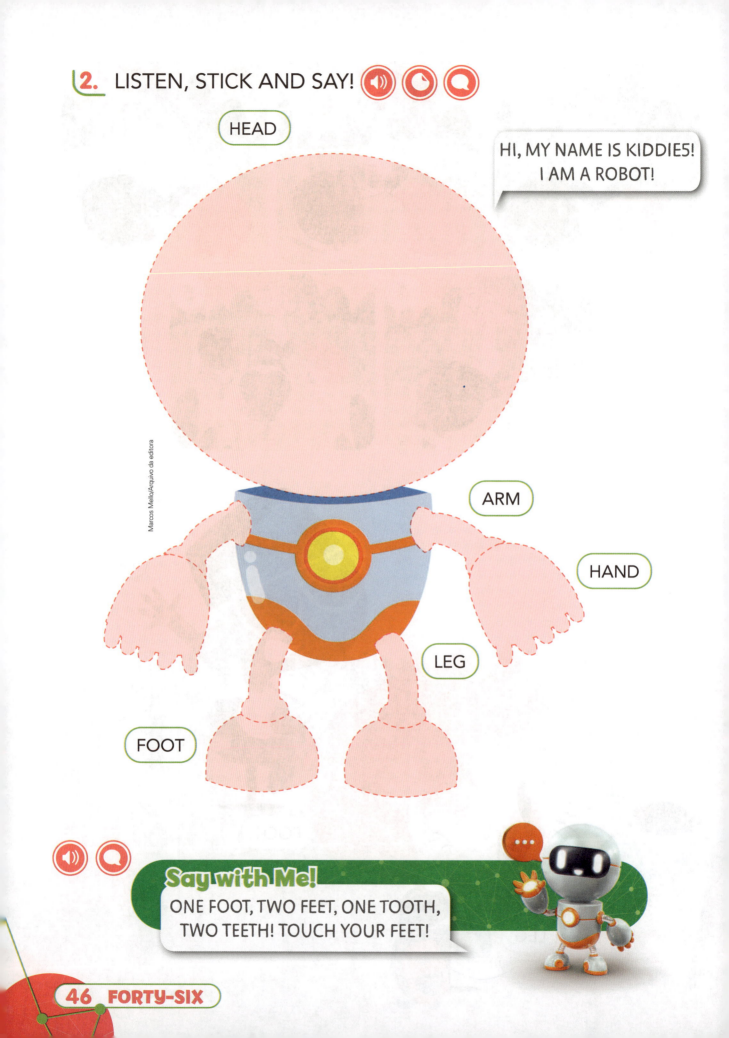

3. LISTEN AND NUMBER THE SEQUENCE.

LET'S SING!

IF YOU'RE HAPPY

IF YOU'RE HAPPY AND YOU KNOW IT,
CLAP YOUR HANDS.
IF YOU'RE HAPPY AND YOU KNOW IT,
CLAP YOUR HANDS.
IF YOU'RE HAPPY AND YOU KNOW IT,
AND YOU REALLY WANT TO SHOW IT
IF YOU'RE HAPPY AND YOU KNOW IT,
CLAP YOUR HANDS.

SNAP YOUR FINGERS.
STAMP YOUR FEET.
DO ALL THREE.

4. MATCH

GROWING UP

NO PREJUDICE

5. LOOK AT THE PICTURE AND TALK TO YOUR CLASSMATES.

6. THINK AND DRAW: "IT'S OK TO BE OR FEEL DIFFERENT".

CHECK YOUR PROGRESS

TIME TO LEARN ABOUT MY BODY

IS YOUR **BODY** HEALTHY?

1. LOOK, THINK AND MAKE AN **X**.

50 FIFTY

I HAVE A HEALTHY BODY!

2. LOOK AND NUMBER THE PICTURES 1 TO 6.

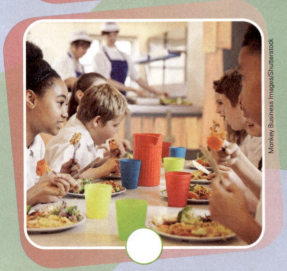 

2. LISTEN, STICK AND SAY!

3. LISTEN AND CIRCLE.

A)

B)

C)

D)

E)

Say with Me!
BUTTERFLIES FLY, FLY! BIRDS FLY, FLY, HIGH IN THE SKY!

4. FIND AND COUNT.

5. MATCH THE PUZZLE.

LET'S SING!

THE PARK RAP

A: GREEN TREES?
B: GREEN TREES.
A: YELLOW BIRDS?
B: YELLOW BIRDS.
A: MANY FLOWERS?
B: MANY FLOWERS.
B: GUESS WHAT?
A: A PARK!
B: YOU'RE RIGHT!
B: YES, A PARK!

6. COLOR AND SAY.

GROWING UP

RESPECT NATURE

7. LOOK AT THE PICTURE AND TALK TO YOUR CLASSMATES.

8. THINK OF ONE WAY TO PRESERVE PARKS AND RESPECT NATURE. DRAW AND ACT IT OUT.

CHECK YOUR PROGRESS

AWESOME!    GOOD JOB!    I CAN DO BETTER.

REVIEW

1. COLOR BY NUMBER.

✦	✦	✦	✦	✦
1	2	3	4	5
PURPLE	PINK	YELLOW	BLUE	RED

2. CHECK. ✓

AT THE PARK HUNT:

FLOWER ○　　CAT ○

KITE ○　　SCHOOLBAG ○

TREE ○　　DOG ○

BOOK ○　　BUTTERFLY ○

BIRD ○　　ICE CREAM ○

UNIT 7 THE GREEN CAP

1. LISTEN, POINT AND SAY.

LOOK AT THE GREEN CAP!

OH! IT'S COOL!

2. LISTEN, STICK AND SAY.

CAP

T-SHIRT

PANTS

SNEAKERS

DRESS

SNEAKERS AND SOCKS

Say with Me!
THIS IS SHIRA'S SHORT, SHINY DRESS.

64 SIXTY-FOUR

3. LISTEN AND COLOR.

LET'S SING!

MY CLOTHES

I LOVE MY CLOTHES.
CLAP, CLAP, CLAP.
T-SHIRTS AND CAPS.
CLAP, CLAP, CLAP.
I LOVE MY CLOTHES.
CLAP, CLAP, CLAP.
SNEAKERS AND SOCKS.
CLAP, CLAP, CLAP.
SNEAKERS, T-SHIRTS, SOCKS AND CAPS.
CLAP, CLAP, CLAP, CLAP, CLAP, CLAP.

4. LISTEN AND CIRCLE.

Ruslan Kudrin/Shutterstock

Karina Bakalyan/Shutterstock

Anton Starikov/Shutterstock

Nadezda/Shutterstock

Lifestyle Travel Photo/Shutterstock

Irina Rogova/Shutterstock

NYS/Shutterstock

GROWING UP

SOLIDARITY

5. LOOK AT THE PICTURE AND TALK TO YOUR CLASSMATES.

6. DO YOU DO SOLIDARITY ACTIONS? DRAW ONE AND SHARE WITH A CLASSMATE.

CHECK YOUR PROGRESS

AWESOME!

GOOD JOB!

I CAN DO BETTER.

TIME TO LEARN ABOUT CLOTHES

ARE YOU CAREFUL WITH YOUR CLOTHES?

1. LOOK, THINK AND COMPLETE THE DRAWING.

I'M CAREFUL WITH MY CLOTHES!

2. LOOK AT THE PICTURES. IN GROUP, FIND A SOLUTION FOR THE PROBLEM AND MATCH.

2. LISTEN, STICK AND SAY!

3. LISTEN AND MAKE AN X.

SEVENTY-THREE 73

4. COMPLETE THE SEQUENCE AND COLOR.

A)

B)

C)

D)

5. WHAT IS YOUR FAVORITE FOOD?

LET'S SING!

THE SHOP LIST CHANT

TAKE THE SHOP LIST.
BANANAS AND COOKIES,
MILK AND CHOCOLATE,
APPLES AND EGGS
AND ORANGE JUICE.
WHAT A LONG LIST!
DO YOU HAVE MONEY?

6. LISTEN AND MAKE AN **X**.

Say with Me!

THIS IS MY SHOP LIST. IT'S NOT SHORT! OH! IT'S LONG!

GROWING UP

NO FOOD WASTE!

7. LOOK AT THE PICTURE AND TALK TO YOUR CLASSMATES.

8. THINK OF FOOD WASTE AND DRAW YOUR PLATE AND FOOD.

CHECK YOUR PROGRESS

AWESOME!   GOOD JOB!   I CAN DO BETTER.

REVIEW

1. DRAW AND COLOR.

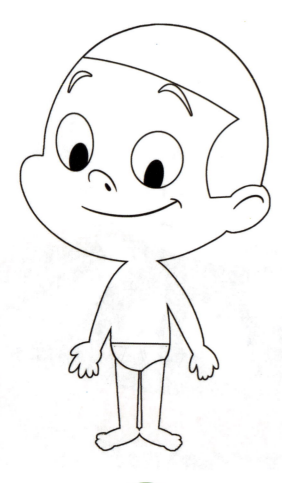

YELLOW T-SHIRT
BROWN PANTS

ORANGE SNEAKERS

RED DRESS

PINK SNEAKERS

2. FIND AND CIRCLE.

6 APPLES

4 EGGS

3 CARTONS OF MILK

5 BANANAS

1 CHOCOLATE BAR

2 BOXES OF COOKIES

2. LISTEN, STICK AND SAY.

A BEAUTIFUL DAY AT THE BEACH!

3. COUNT AND COLOR.

LET'S SING!

LET'S GO TO THE BEACH!

A: IT'S SUMMER!
B: IT'S SUMMER!
A: THE SUN IS SHINING.
B: THE SUN IS SHINING.
A: THE SKY IS BLUE.
B: THE SKY IS BLUE.
A: LET'S GO TO THE BEACH!
B: LET'S GO TO THE BEACH!
A: LET'S GO TO THE BEACH!

4. DRAW AND SAY.

Say with Me!
STARFISH, STARFISH, I WISH
I SEE A STARFISH.

GROWING UP

PROTECT THE OCEAN

5. LOOK AT THE PICTURE AND TALK TO YOUR CLASSMATES.

6. THINK OF ACTIONS TO PRESERVE BEACHES AND OCEANS. MIME IT AND ASK YOUR CLASSMATES TO GUESS. THEN DRAW THE ACTION.

CHECK YOUR PROGRESS

AWESOME!	GOOD JOB!	I CAN DO BETTER.

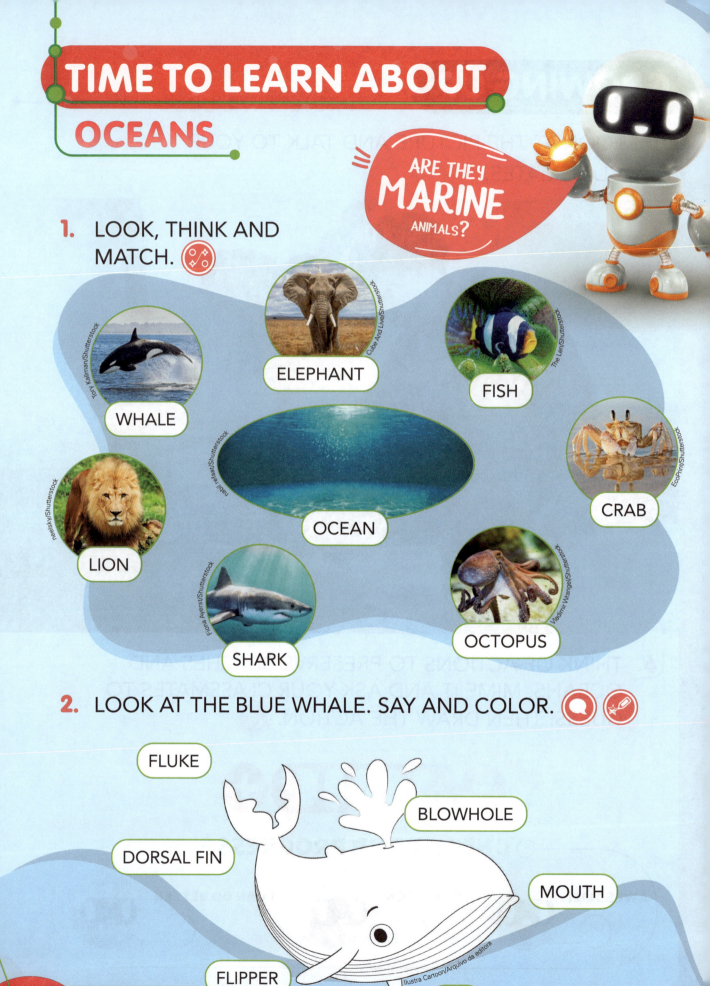

THIS IS MY BLUE WHALE!

3. LET'S CREATE YOUR OWN BLUE WHALE.

COLORED PENS

SCISSORS

BLUE CARDBOARD

BLACK MARKER

GLUE STICK

BLUE PAINT AND BRUSH

PAPER PLATE

UNIT 10

ON THE FARM

1. LISTEN, POINT AND SAY.

2. LISTEN, STICK AND SAY.

3. LISTEN AND MAKE AN **X**.

A)

B)

C)

D)

4. FIND 6 DIFFERENCES.

5. CIRCLE AND COLOR THE FARM ANIMALS.

LET'S SING!

OLD MACDONALD HAD A FARM

OLD MACDONALD
HAD A FARM
E – I – E – I – O
AND ON HIS FARM
HE HAD A COW
E – I – E – I – O
WITH A MOO MOO HERE
AND A MOO MOO THERE
HERE A MOO, THERE A MOO,
EVERYWHERE A MOO MOO

OLD MACDONALD HAD A FARM
E – I – E – I – O
AND ON HIS FARM HE HAD A PIG
E – I – E – I – O
WITH A OINK OINK HERE
AND A OINK OINK THERE
HERE A OINK, THERE A OINK
EVERYWHERE A OINK OINK
OLD MACDONALD HAD A FARM
E – I – E – I – O
(CONTINUE)

6. LISTEN AND CIRCLE.

Say with Me!
THE CHARMER FARMER HAS A FARM, A HORSE AND A HEN!

GROWING UP

PROTECT THE ANIMALS

7. LOOK AT THE PICTURE AND TALK TO YOUR CLASSMATES.

Catalin Petolea/Shutterstock

8. THINK OF WAYS TO PROTECT, RESPECT AND CARE FOR ANIMALS. DRAW ONE AND ACT IT OUT.

CHECK YOUR PROGRESS

AWESOME!

GOOD JOB!

I CAN DO BETTER.

REVIEW

1. WRITE THE LETTERS.

BOAT

F ___ S H

S ___ ___ S H ___ L L

S T ___ F ___ ___ H

S ___ N

___ ___ O V ___ ___

B ___ ___ K E ___

2. NUMBER.

HORSE ◯   HEN ◯   COW ◯

DUCK ◯   CHICK ◯   PIG ◯

NINETY-SEVEN 97

PROJECT 1 — COLORS ARE EVERYWHERE!

1. LOOK AT THE PICTURES. WHAT COLORS CAN YOU SEE?

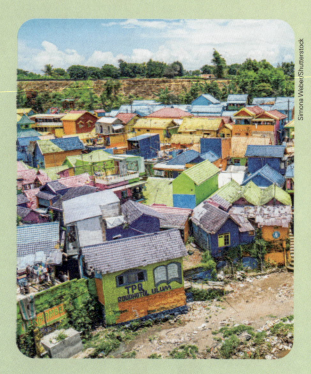

2. CAN COLORS EXPRESS HOW YOU FEEL? LET'S TRY! WHAT COLOR MAKES YOU FEEL:

 A — CALM

 D — SLEEPY

 B — HAPPY

 E — SURPRISED

 C — SAD

 F — AFRAID

3. ARTISTS USE COLORS TO CREATE THEIR WORKS. WHAT COLORS CAN YOU SEE? ✓

SEM TÍTULO, DE TOMIE OHTAKE, 1954 (ÓLEO SOBRE TELA, 46 cm × 76 cm).

SEM TÍTULO, DE TOMIE OHTAKE, 1974 (ÓLEO SOBRE TELA, 165 cm × 165 cm).

- BLACK
- GREEN
- PINK
- RED
- PURPLE
- WHITE
- BLUE
- GRAY
- BROWN
- YELLOW
- ORANGE

4. DRAW YOUR OWN PAINTING TO EXPRESS HOW YOU FEEL DURING A HOT DAY AND A COLD ONE. CREATE AN ART GALLERY.

PROJECT 2 BABY ANIMALS

1. LOOK AT THE PICTURES. WHAT ARE THEIR NAMES?

2. WHAT ANIMAL IS IT?

100 ONE HUNDRED

3. COLOR AND MATCH THE BABY ANIMALS TO THEIR MOTHERS.

4. IN GROUP, CREATE A MODEL OF THE ANIMALS WITH PLAY DOUGH. THEN PLAY WITH THEM.

PICTURE DICTIONARY

A

APPLE

ARM

B

BABY

BALL

BANANAS

BEACH

BIKE

BIRD

BLUE

BOAT

BOOK

BOY

BROWN

BUCKET

BUTTERFLY

C

CAP

CAR

CAT

CHICK

CHOCOLATE

CIRCLE

CLASSROOM

COMPUTER

COOKIES

COW

CRAYON

DOG

DOLL

DRESS

DUCK

EGG

EIGHT

ERASER

FINGER

FISH

FIVE

FLOWER

FOOT

ONE HUNDRED AND THREE 103

FOUR

GIRL

GREEN

HAND

HEAD

HEN

HORSE

ICE CREAM

JUICE

LEG

MILK

NINE

OMELET

ONE

ORANGE

PANTS

PARK

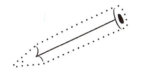
PENCIL

PIG

PINK

RED

SANDCASTLE

SCHOOL

SCHOOLBAG

SCHOOL BUS

SEA

SEESAW

SEASHELL

SHOVEL

SIX

SKY

SLIDE

SNEAKERS

SOCKS

SQUARE

STARFISH

STORE

ONE HUNDRED AND FIVE 105

STUDENT

SUN

SUNSCREEN

SWING

TABLET

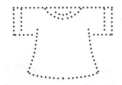
T-SHIRT

TEACHER

TEN

THREE

TOES

TREE

TRIANGLE

TV

TWO

VIDEO GAME

WATER

YELLOW

106 ONE HUNDRED AND SIX

UNIT 1 — MY FAMILY

NAME: _____

CLASS: _____ **DATE:** ___/___/___

1. CIRCLE AND COLOR THE ODD ONE OUT.

ONE HUNDRED AND SEVEN 107

2. DOT TO DOT AND MATCH.

- LEO
- FIDO

3. MATCH.

UNIT 2 — WELCOME, TEACHER!

NAME: _____

CLASS: _____ **DATE:** ___/___/___

1. MATCH.

2. DRAW AND COLOR.

PAY ATTENTION!

3. MATCH.

110 ONE HUNDRED AND TEN

UNIT 3 ART CLASS

NAME: _____

CLASS: _____ DATE: ___/___/___

1. COLOR.

ONE HUNDRED AND ELEVEN 111

2. DRAW AND COLOR.

3. COLOR AND CIRCLE.

WHAT COLOR IS IT?

IT IS...

- BLUE
- BROWN
- GREEN
- ORANGE
- PINK
- RED
- YELLOW

UNIT 4 — LET'S PLAY HOPSCOTCH!

NAME: _____

CLASS: _____ DATE: ____/____/____

1. COUNT THE STARS AND MATCH.

WORKBOOK

ONE HUNDRED AND THIRTEEN 113

2. COUNT, DRAW AND COMPLETE.

3. COUNT AND CIRCLE.

| TEN – TWO THREE | FIVE – TWO FOUR | FIVE TWO – EIGHT | TWO NINE – ONE |

UNIT 5 — SHOW ME YOUR ARMS

NAME: _____

CLASS: _____ DATE: ___/___/___

1. DRAW.

HI! THIS IS SMOG #THE MONSTER. HE HAS THREE ARMS, THREE HANDS, ONE FOOT AND ONE HEAD.

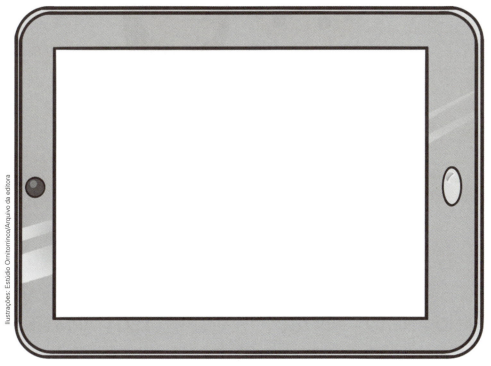

ONE HUNDRED AND FIFTEEN 115

2. MATCH.

• HI!

• ARE YOU OK?

3. CIRCLE.

HAND – HEAD – FOOT   LEG – ARM – HAND

UNIT 6 AT THE PARK

NAME: _____

CLASS: _____ **DATE:** ___/___/___

1. MATCH AND COLOR.

ONE HUNDRED AND SEVENTEEN 117

2. CIRCLE.

3. NUMBER THE JIGSAW PIECES.

118 ONE HUNDRED AND EIGHTEEN

UNIT 7 THE GREEN CAP

NAME: _____

CLASS: _____ DATE: ___ / ___ / ___

1. MATCH.

2. MAKE AN X.

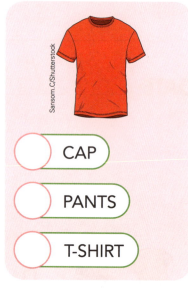
- ◯ CAP
- ◯ PANTS
- ◯ T-SHIRT

- ◯ DRESS
- ◯ PANTS
- ◯ SNEAKERS

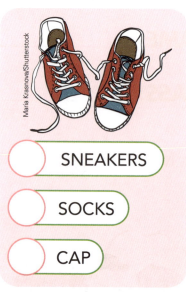
- ◯ SNEAKERS
- ◯ SOCKS
- ◯ CAP

- ◯ DRESS
- ◯ SCHOOLBAG
- ◯ SHOES

- ◯ SHOES
- ◯ CAP
- ◯ SOCKS

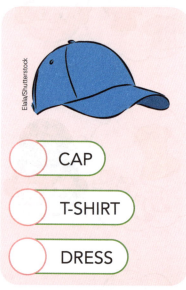
- ◯ CAP
- ◯ T-SHIRT
- ◯ DRESS

- ◯ PANTS
- ◯ SCHOOLBAG
- ◯ DRESS

- ◯ SHOES
- ◯ T-SHIRT
- ◯ PANTS

- ◯ SHORTS
- ◯ SHOES
- ◯ SCHOOLBAG

UNIT 8 — I LIKE COOKIES!

NAME: _____

CLASS: _____ DATE: ____/____/____

1. MAKE AN ✘ OR ✔.

2. CIRCLE 5 DIFFERENCES.

3. COLOR.

WHAT IS YOUR FAVORITE FOOD?
I LOVE...

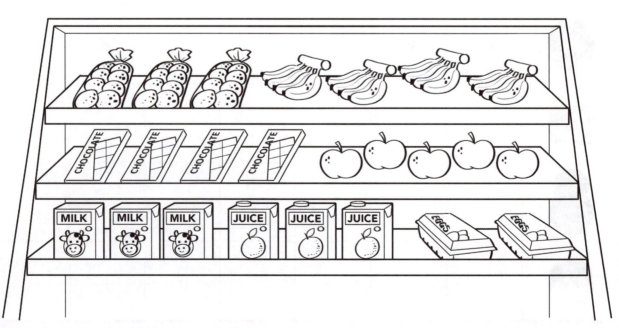

UNIT 9 — AT THE BEACH

NAME: _____

CLASS: _____ DATE: ___/___/___

1. NUMBER.

1 BOAT   4 SEASHELL   7 SUN
2 FISH   5 SKY   8 SANDCASTLE
3 SEA   6 STARFISH   9 BUCKET

ONE HUNDRED AND TWENTY-THREE 123

2. FIND AND COLOR.

WHERE ARE THE  AND THE ?

3. DRAW.

IT'S A BEAUTIFUL DAY!

UNIT 10 ON THE FARM

NAME: _____

CLASS: _____ DATE: ___/___/___

1. ODD ONE OUT.

2. DRAW AND COLOR.

WHERE IS THE DUCK ?

WHERE IS THE CHICK ?

WHERE IS THE HORSE?

3. MATCH.

CELEBRATION SONGS

HAPPY BIRTHDAY

HAPPY BIRTHDAY TO YOU!
HAPPY BIRTHDAY TO YOU!
HAPPY BIRTHDAY, DEAR...!
HAPPY BIRTHDAY TO YOU!

EASTER BUNNY

EASTER BUNNY,
EASTER BUNNY,
WHAT DO YOU BRING TO ME?
ONE EGG, TWO EGGS, THREE EGGS, SO, SO!
ONE EGG, TWO EGGS, THREE EGGS, SO, SO!

DEAR MOM!

MY DEAR MOM,
SO SWEET,
SO BEAUTIFUL...
YOU'RE SO LOVELY!
YOU'RE ALL TO ME!

MY HERO!

MY DAD IS SO COOL.
MY DAD IS SO BRAVE.
MY DAD IS MY FRIEND.
OH, MY DAD,
YOU ARE MY HERO!

MR. TURKEY

MR. TURKEY, MR. TURKEY,
RUN AWAY, RUN AWAY.
PLEASE, BE CAREFUL,
IT'S THANKSGIVING DAY.

WE WISH YOU A MERRY CHRISTMAS

WE WISH YOU A MERRY CHRISTMAS,
WE WISH YOU A MERRY CHRISTMAS,
WE WISH YOU A MERRY CHRISTMAS
AND A HAPPY NEW YEAR!

CELEBRATION CRAFTS

HAPPY EASTER!

MOTHER'S DAY

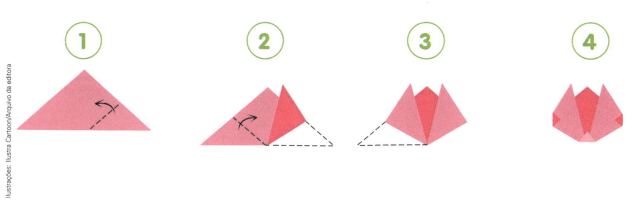

FATHER'S DAY

FRIENDSHIP DAY

ONE HUNDRED AND THIRTY-THREE 133

_____, OUR FRIENDSHIP IS SWEETER THAN CANDY.

THANKSGIVING DAY

CHRISTMAS

138 ONE HUNDRED AND THIRTY-EIGHT

GAME

MEMORY GAME

MINI CARDS

INSTRUÇÕES
- O ENVELOPE E AS MINICARTAS DEVEM SER DESTACADOS COM CUIDADO.
- DEPOIS DE DESTACADO DA FOLHA, O ENVELOPE DEVE SER DOBRADO E COLADO NOS LOCAIS INDICADOS. NELE SERÃO GUARDADAS AS MINICARTAS.

——— DOBRE
-------- DESTAQUE

HELLO! KIDS 1

MINI CARDS

Material integrante da Coleção **Hello! Kids 1**
Eliete Canesi Morino • Rita Brugin de Faria
Reprodução e venda proibidas

ea editora ática

GLUE   GLUE

ea editora ática

NAME:

ONE HUNDRED AND FORTY-ONE 141

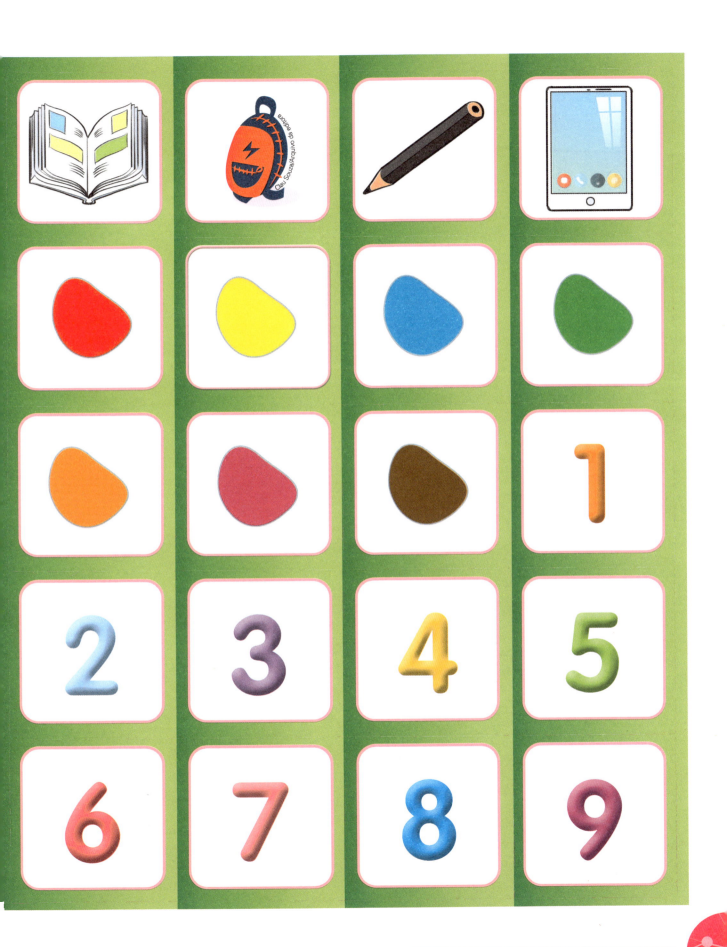

STICKERS

NAME: _____
CLASS: _____

NAME: _____
CLASS: _____

PAGES 6 AND 7

PAGES 8 AND 9

PAGES 16 AND 17

PAGE 10

PAGE 18

PAGE 28

ONE HUNDRED AND FORTY-NINE 149

PAGES 26 AND 27

PAGES 34 AND 35

PAGES 44 AND 45

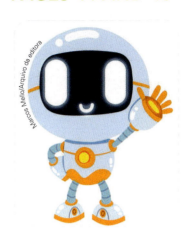

PAGE 36

PAGE 46

PAGE 54

PAGES 52 AND 53

PAGES 62 AND 63

PAGE 64

PAGES 70 AND 71

PAGE 72

PAGE 82

PAGES 80 AND 81

PAGE 90

PAGES 88 AND 89

ONE HUNDRED AND FIFTY-FIVE 155